UNFORGETTABLE
NATURAL DISASTERS

Tamara Leigh Hollingsworth

Consultants

Timothy Rasinski, Ph.D.
Kent State University

Lori Oczkus
Literacy Consultant

Based on writing from
TIME For Kids. *TIME For Kids* and the *TIME For Kids* logo are registered trademarks of TIME Inc. Used under license.

Publishing Credits

Dona Herweck Rice, *Editor-in-Chief*
Lee Aucoin, *Creative Director*
Jamey Acosta, *Senior Editor*
Heidi Fiedler, *Editor*
Lexa Hoang, *Designer*
Stephanie Reid, *Photo Editor*
Rane Anderson, *Contributing Author*
Rachelle Cracchiolo, *M.S.Ed., Publisher*

Image Credits: p.19 Alamy; p.25 Associated Press; p.44 The Bridgeman Art Library; pp.44–45, 46 Corbis; pp.28–29 Encyclopædia Britannica, Inc.; pp.33, 38, 50–51 Getty Images/Science Faction; p.54 CDC.gov; pp.26, 53 (bottom) Library of Congress; pp.46–47 Thomas Coex/AFP/Getty Images/Newscom; p.5 Stan Honda/AFP/Getty Images/Newscom; p.39 Yasuyoshi Chiba/AFP/Getty Images/Newscom; p.7 Made Nagi/EPA/Newscom; p.41 (bottom) imagebroker/Michael Dietrich/Newscom; pp.26–27 Tom Van Dyke/MCT/Newscom; pp.6–7 Thomas Peter/Reuters/Newscom; p.30 Baz Ratner/Reuters/Newscom; pp.18–19 Supri/Reuters/Newscom; p.24 Newscom; p.4 Eddie Mejia/Splash News/Newscom; p.53 (top) wenn.com/Newscom; p.56 Zuma Press/Newscom; p.41 (top) Zuma Press/Newscom; pp.23, 40–41 Gary Hincks/Photo Researchers Inc.; pp.16 (bottom), 17 (bottom), 55 (illustrations) John Schahill; pp.16–17, 22 (illustrations) Timothy J. Bradley; All other images from Shutterstock.

Teacher Created Materials

5301 Oceanus Drive
Huntington Beach, CA 92649-1030
http://www.tcmpub.com

ISBN 978-1-4333-7494-7
© 2013 Teacher Created Materials, Inc.

TABLE OF CONTENTS

LIFE IN THE DANGER ZONE

When a disaster hits, it can be hard to find food. Houses may be without running water. In fact, the houses themselves may have been destroyed. There may be nowhere to live, nowhere to sleep, and nothing to eat. Disasters can be scary, but the ways they bring people together can be unforgettable.

Victims of the 2010 Haitian earthquake wait for help to arrive.

A volunteer hands out sandwiches to children who lost their homes during Hurricane Katrina in 2005.

THINK LINK

› How do disasters affect the world?

› How can we predict when the next disaster will occur?

› How can we survive disasters in the future?

Natural disasters can happen anytime, anywhere. What's the best way to avoid a disaster? Know when one is coming! Progress has been made in predicting disasters. Scientists track weather patterns. They watch for impending floods and hurricanes. But when it comes to predicting earthquakes and volcanic **eruptions**, it gets more difficult. Often, they occur without any warning.

Natural disasters will continue to affect us no matter what we do. But we can prepare for them. And when the worst happens, we can work together to rebuild what was lost.

> "I beg you take courage; the brave soul can mend even disaster."
>
> —Catherine the Great, Russian Empress

CHARTING TREMORS

Scientists map earthquakes and their aftershocks, the small earthquakes that often happen after a huge one. This helps them predict and reduce damage during the next disaster.

Rescue teams prepare for disasters by practicing rescues.

Ho Ch

Singapore

Palembang

Jakarta
Ban

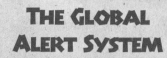

THE GLOBAL ALERT SYSTEM

If a disaster is **imminent**, we want to know about it. That is why the Global Disaster Alert and Coordination System (GDACS) was created. The GDACS tracks the weather and gathers data from around the world. It monitors earthquakes, water levels, and wind speeds. Scientists study the data and make predictions. Then, they alert people when a disaster may be coming. These alerts give up-to-date information before and after a disaster hits.

GDACS tracks a variety of disasters. Symbols show what places are in danger.

 Earthquakes

 Volcano

Tropical cyclone

Flood

Even an hour's warning can give people in the danger zone time to prepare or escape to safety.

DANGER FROM ABOVE

The night sky is home to millions of stars. In their midst, rocks and metals are speeding toward Earth in the form of "shooting stars." Some of these **meteors** are small and burn up in our atmosphere. Others strike the Earth, forming craters. There are also asteroids flying toward us. Scientists watch for these "falling stars." They try to predict where they will land next so they can prevent serious damage. Astronomers also watch for comets. These huge balls of rock and ice could be deadly if they struck Earth. The danger is remote, though. Getting hit by a deadly meteor is less likely than winning the lottery. It's less likely than receiving an Oscar. Or becoming an astronaut! And scientists are watching the skies closely to help us avoid disaster.

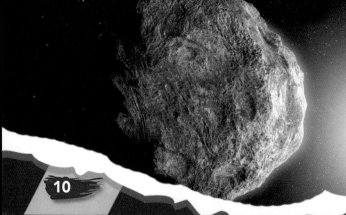

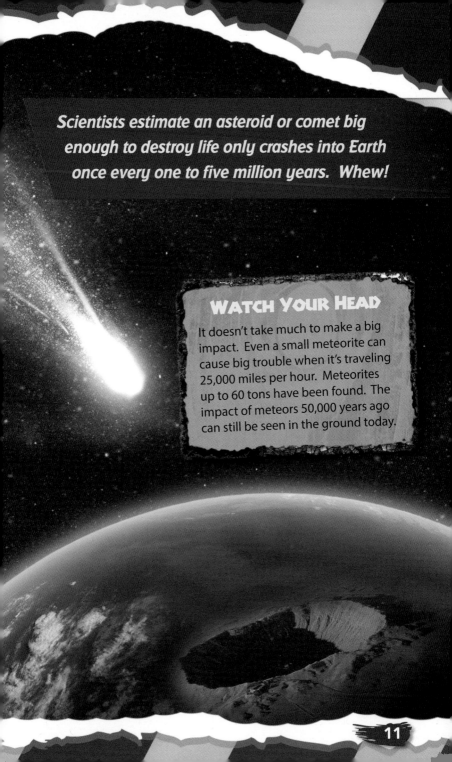

Scientists estimate an asteroid or comet big enough to destroy life only crashes into Earth once every one to five million years. Whew!

WATCH YOUR HEAD

It doesn't take much to make a big impact. Even a small meteorite can cause big trouble when it's traveling 25,000 miles per hour. Meteorites up to 60 tons have been found. The impact of meteors 50,000 years ago can still be seen in the ground today.

Dinosaur Disaster

Seventy million years ago, dinosaurs ruled the world, but everything changed when a huge meteor hit Earth. The impact caused a **massive** dust cloud. The dust darkened the sky and hid the sun for months. Plant life died without the sun's light. The dark days left plant-eating dinosaurs without food, and they couldn't survive. When the plant-eating dinosaurs died, it left no food for the others. Soon, even the larger meat-eating dinosaurs died off, too. They became extinct, but smaller creatures like mammals survived. They became the new rulers of the land. Today, humans—the most intelligent mammals in the world—dominate.

CHICXULUB CRATER

In the 1970s, a deep, wide crater was discovered in the city of Chicxulub in Mexico. After decades of research, most scientists concluded it is the landing spot of the meteor that killed the dinosaurs.

FROM POWERLESS TO POWERFUL

During the time of the dinosaurs, the only mammals were rodents, similar to rats. If dinosaurs had survived, it's possible they might still rule the natural world and humans may never have evolved.

TROUBLE FROM BELOW

Some disasters rumble, shake, and rip the ground we stand on. Others spew molten lava and rock high in the sky, make huge clouds of ash, and melt everything they touch. Earthquakes and volcanoes start underground, but the havoc they wreak happens on the ground where we live.

Volcanoes

A powerful volcanic eruption can bury a whole city, and a massive eruption has the power to wipe out humankind. The danger lies deep in the Earth's layers.

We build our homes on Earth's crust, the top layer. The crust is made up of pieces that are different shapes and sizes. These large pieces of the crust are called **plates**. Volcanoes form in the space where the plates meet, just as a weed grows out of a crack in the cement. Hot lava, **magma**, and gases escape between these cracks to create a volcano. When too much pressure forms, volcanoes erupt, throwing burning lava, dangerous gases, and hot ash into the air. An eruption can cause serious damage to the surrounding areas. Scientists work with governments to warn people and prevent the most serious damage.

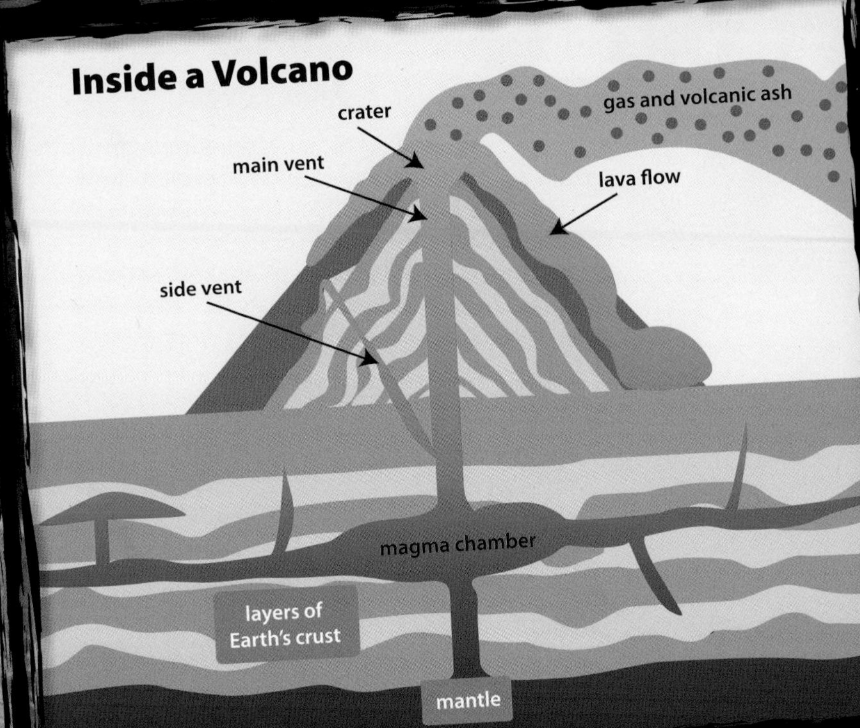

Inside a Volcano

crater

main vent

side vent

gas and volcanic ash

lava flow

magma chamber

layers of Earth's crust

mantle

MOLTEN MAGMA

Volcanoes look like ordinary mountains, but they have activity inside them that regular mountains do not. Volcanoes are filled with magma. When a volcano erupts, it spits out pieces of rock and magma. Once the magma comes out of the top, it is called *lava*.

DIG DEEPER!

A MAZE OF MAGMA

Quick! A volcano is erupting, and there's only one way to escape. Take a look at the three types of volcanoes described at the bottom of the page. Then, identify the different types of volcanoes to make your way through the maze of magma. Hurry! You don't have much time before the lava reaches you.

START

Cinder Cones
These round volcanoes simmer quietly. They release small hard pieces of lava.

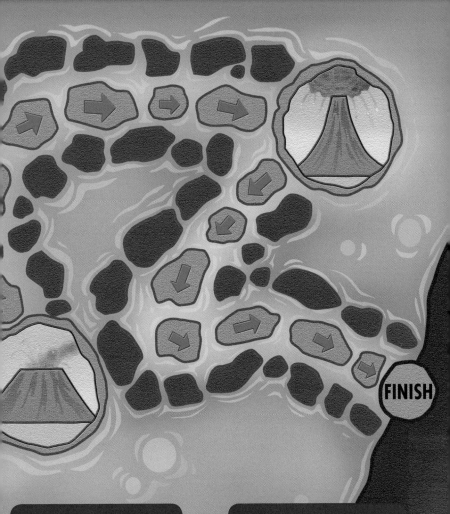

FINISH

Composite Volcanoes
These volcanoes are tall and violent. They throw ash, rock, and lava great distances when they erupt.

Shield Volcanoes
These volcanoes are wide and squat. Lava flows gently from the top.

Answer: 1) shield   2) cinder   3) composite

Krakatoa

Boom! Like many islands, Krakatoa was formed from a volcano. A million years later, in 1883, the volcano erupted again. The thunderous eruption was heard 2,200 miles away. People were surprised because the volcano had been peaceful for more than 200 years. They didn't think there would be any danger. The powerful blast formed a cloud of ash that blocked the sun for 180 miles. **Debris** fell over 300,000 square miles. It took three years for the dust to settle. Two thirds of the island was destroyed.

VOLCANIC ISLANDS

Underwater volcanoes erupt and produce streams of fiery, hot lava. The hardened lava forms new islands. The Hawaiian Islands were formed that way.

New Dimensions

These maps show how the island of Krakatoa changed after the eruption. The shape of the land changed and the depth of the ocean changed as well.

Scale 1 : 150,000

Depths:

0 to 160 feet	160 to 320 feet	320 feet and deeper

KRAKATOA BEFORE

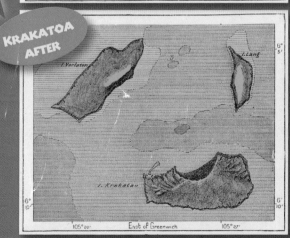

KRAKATOA AFTER

Mount St. Helens

Volcanoes can be found on continents as well as on islands. The United States is home to Mount St. Helens in Washington State. Just 100 miles south of Seattle, it is still active. In 1980, an earthquake changed the pressure inside Mount St. Helens. That caused the north side to bulge. Two months later, another earthquake led to an eruption that lasted nine hours. It threw rocks and ash into the air and caused mudslides. Eleven states reported falling volcanic ash. The debris from the explosion destroyed 150 miles of nearby forests. Early warnings helped keep many people safe. Scientists are able to warn of eruptions even earlier now.

The force from the blast of Mount St. Helens flattened trees over a 19 mile area.

HIGH VOLUME VOLCANOES

The noise from an erupting volcano can damage your hearing. When Krakatoa blew its stack, the noise was thunderous. People said anyone within 10 miles was deafened by the sound.

After

Before

VISIT MOUNT ST. HELENS

Today, Mount St. Helens is a national park. Many people visit the park to see the site of a volcanic disaster. Others are more interested in learning about volcanoes. They want to find out how to predict when other volcanoes will erupt.

Earthquakes

Volcanic eruptions are just one kind of disaster that happens under our feet. Sometimes, the plates in the Earth's crust shift. The plates can push, pull, or slide against each other. This movement causes changes in the land we live on. When the plates push together, they create **geographical** features like mountain ranges. When they pull apart, they create space for volcanoes to form. But whenever these plates move, it causes an earthquake.

Earthquakes can cause buildings to collapse. Powerful quakes can even cause a **tsunami** to flood the shore. But technology is improving, and we are finding ways to prevent damage.

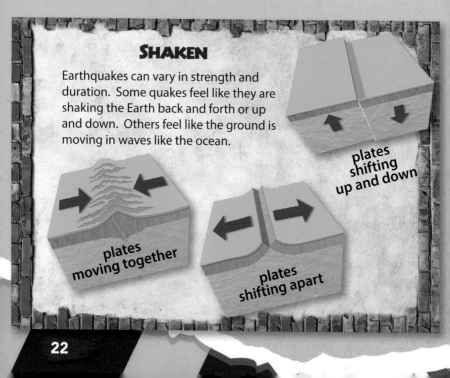

SHAKEN

Earthquakes can vary in strength and duration. Some quakes feel like they are shaking the Earth back and forth or up and down. Others feel like the ground is moving in waves like the ocean.

plates shifting up and down

plates moving together

plates shifting apart

PLATE TECTONICS

After an earthquake, scientists map the movements of the Earth. They look at notes that were made about past earthquakes. They study underwater mountains and valleys. They study the ocean floor. It helps them understand where an earthquake will happen in the future.

The gray lines on this map show many of the world's major fault lines, or boundaries between the Earth's plates. The red dots show major earthquake sites.

Ancient Quakes

The world's deadliest earthquake is believed to have happened in the year 1201. The **epicenter** was in Syria, but the quake was felt many miles away, too. At that time, people didn't design buildings with earthquakes in mind, so the great quake destroyed their towns. Over a million people died. The **magnitude** of the earthquake was 7.6 on the Richter scale. Throughout history, there have been stronger earthquakes. But this quake was felt over a large area, and people were unprepared. This resulted in a high death toll and extreme damage throughout the region. Today, we could survive an earthquake this size.

BUILDING FOR QUAKES

In places where earthquakes are common, such as California and Japan, architects work to improve the strength of their buildings. They reinforce the buildings with stronger materials. They may even try out different shapes for their buildings.

THE RICHTER SCALE

The Richter scale measures the waves of energy created during an earthquake. Thanks to its inventor, Charles Richter, we can rate the strength of an earthquake.

Magnitude	Category	Effects	Earthquakes per Year
1.0–2.9	micro	usually not felt by people	more than 100,000
3.0–3.9	minor	felt by many people, damage is rare	12,000–100,000
4.0–4.9	light	felt by all people, causes small objects to break	2,000–12,000
5.0–5.9	moderate	some damage to weak structures	200–2,000
6.0–6.9	strong	moderate damage in cities and towns	20–200
7.0–7.9	major	serious damage caused over large areas, loss of life	3–20
8.0 and higher	great	severe damage and loss of life over large areas	fewer than 3

The Great Quake

Very early one morning in 1906, the coastline of California shook. The epicenter of the earthquake was just off the coast of San Francisco. Buildings collapsed. Trees were uprooted. Gas pipes cracked and leaked out into the air. A fire spread rapidly through the city. The fire burned for three days and nights. The San Francisco earthquake of 1906 nearly destroyed the city. But because of what happened, **engineers** learned how to build cities that could survive earthquakes.

Sailors on ships a hundred miles away could see the thick smoke of the fires caused by the great earthquake.

A SECOND SHAKE

Can an earthquake that lasts only 10 to 15 seconds do much damage? It can if it's a strong one! In 1989, another earthquake hit San Francisco. It measured a whopping 7.1 on the Richter scale. Major highways and bridges collapsed. Some people were trapped in their cars. Sixty-three people were killed. If we hadn't learned from the 1906 earthquake, more people would have died.

FAULT LINES

When plates in the Earth's crust move, pressure builds. A fault line is where the edges of two different plates touch. Sometimes, the plates bump up against each other. Sometimes, they move in opposite directions. And often, they rub against each other, creating a great amount of friction. The plates can suddenly slip. Any of these movements can cause earthquakes.

EUROPE

ASIA

AFRICA

ATLANTIC
OCEAN

INDIAN
OCEAN

AUSTRALIA

ANTARCTICA

STOP! THINK...

- Where have most earthquakes occurred in the last 25 years?

- Is there a relationship between the depths of the quakes and their strength?

- Is there any relationship between the size of the quakes and their location?

NORTH AMERICA

ATLANTIC OCEAN

PACIFIC OCEAN

Equator

SOUTH AMERICA

Depth of Earthquake

miles
0
21
43
93
186
311
497

Circle size reflects earthquake magnitude.

WHEN YOU LEAST EXPECT IT

Disaster can come from anywhere. Sometimes, the things we need most, like food, water, and the sun's warmth, fail us. Although the dangers can be unexpected, new ways to survive can be found in unexpected places, too.

LONG LASTING DESTRUCTION

Floods continue to destroy even after the water clears. Water damage is extremely destructive. When a car or a home is flooded, almost everything the water touches must be removed and replaced. If water damage is not treated, mold can grow and make people sick.

a flash flood in Israel

Floods

We use water for drinking, cleaning, and cooking. But when water becomes hard to control, it can destroy everything in its path. Floods occur when there is too much water for the ground to **absorb**. During a flood, rivers and creeks can overflow. Water can overtake cities and towns as it covers buildings or bridges. Floodwater moves quickly and can wash away whatever or whoever is in it.

FLASH FLOODS

Flash flooding occurs when heavy rain comes down quickly and then moves on. Because the rain pools so fast, small streams and creeks cannot contain all the water. They aren't as common as floods, but flash floods can be just as deadly if they catch people off guard.

A Deadly Summer

In the winter of 1931, the worst flood in modern history poured through China. The snow that year was heavy. When it **thawed** in the spring, there was **excess** water in the major rivers. China's Yellow River, Yangtze River, and Huai River were full before the heavy rains began in summer. It rained over two feet in August alone. As a result, all three rivers rose. It started to flood. The flood covered a massive area. Diseases spread in the moist environment. More than four million people died from the flood. Today, doctors know how to prevent these types of diseases. Flood victims are moved to clean, dry areas quickly.

CONSTANT BATTLE

When people create cities near powerful rivers, they often battle with flooding. Cities in Egypt must contend with the Nile River. In the United States, flooding occurs on the Mississippi River. In each place, people have developed ways to predict and survive flooding.

The Yellow River gets its name from the fine yellow dirt in it.

Rescuers bring food to people stuck in their houses after a flood.

CRADLE OF CHINA

The Yellow River isn't the largest river in China. But for the Chinese, it is the most important. The Chinese believe the spirit of their people and their culture flow from this river. Many important temples, empires, and people built their lives and customs at the base of the river.

the Yellow River in China

Hurricane Katrina

Rivers aren't the only source of wet disasters. In 2005, a hurricane hit the southern coast of the United States. Hurricanes start over the ocean with strong winds and blinding rains. Then, **storm surges** hit the coast. These powerful waves of water are stirred up by the hurricane.

When Hurricane Katrina flooded the South, the rain and winds caused major damage. Houses were torn from the ground and lakes overflowed with water, but the flooding that came from the storm surge did the most damage. It left many cities along the coast completely underwater. The damage from Katrina is thought to have cost over $80 billion dollars.

FRANKENSTORM

Days before Halloween in October 2012, Hurricane Sandy met up with another storm system before it made landfall in the New York and New Jersey areas. **Meteorologists** called it *Superstorm Sandy* and warned everyone in its path to **evacuate** and prepare for the worst. Because warnings allowed advance notice, schools, airports, and train stations were closed. People were able to move to safer areas where they could stock up on supplies and wait until their homes were safe to go back to.

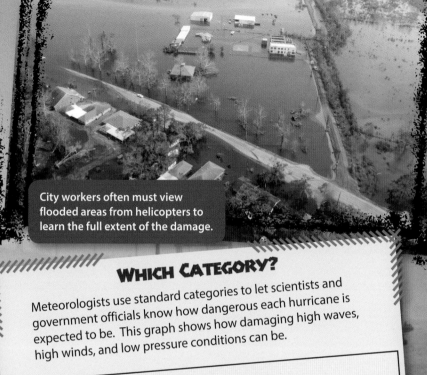

City workers often must view flooded areas from helicopters to learn the full extent of the damage.

WHICH CATEGORY?

Meteorologists use standard categories to let scientists and government officials know how dangerous each hurricane is expected to be. This graph shows how damaging high waves, high winds, and low pressure conditions can be.

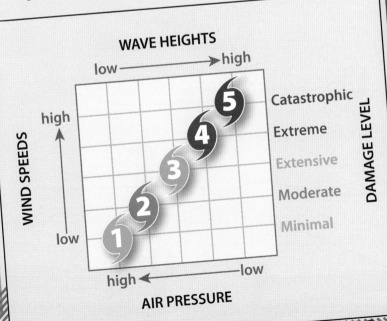

WAVE HEIGHTS

low ➔ high

WIND SPEEDS

high

low

AIR PRESSURE

high ← low

DAMAGE LEVEL

Catastrophic

Extreme

Extensive

Moderate

Minimal

5
4
3
2
1

Tsunami!

Sometimes, an earthquake or volcanic eruption is not the end of the story. Either one can trigger a tsunami. When the Earth shakes, the ocean is affected as well. Huge **tidal waves** wash over the land. These waves can cause the same damage as a flood. Tsunamis are among the worst disasters. The land is already hurt from the volcano or earthquake, and then it is flooded by the waters of the tsunami.

HOW A TSUNAMI FORMS

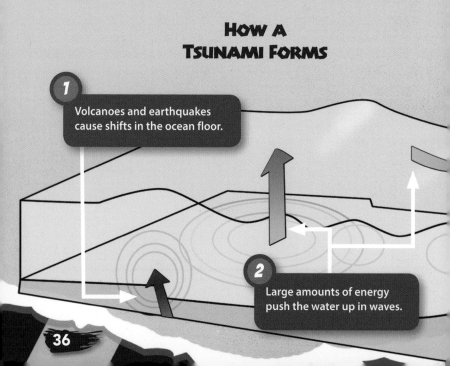

1 Volcanoes and earthquakes cause shifts in the ocean floor.

2 Large amounts of energy push the water up in waves.

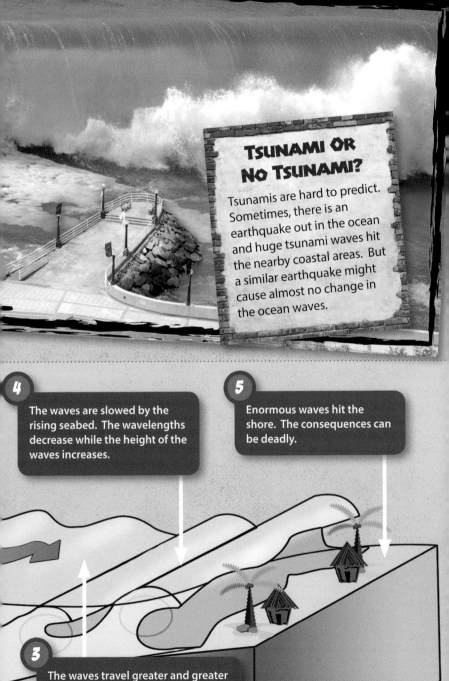

TSUNAMI OR NO TSUNAMI?

Tsunamis are hard to predict. Sometimes, there is an earthquake out in the ocean and huge tsunami waves hit the nearby coastal areas. But a similar earthquake might cause almost no change in the ocean waves.

4

The waves are slowed by the rising seabed. The wavelengths decrease while the height of the waves increases.

5

Enormous waves hit the shore. The consequences can be deadly.

3

The waves travel greater and greater distances as the energy builds.

Japanese Tsunami

March 11, 2011, marked one of the worst natural disasters for Japan. On that day, both an earthquake and a tsunami hit. It was the most powerful earthquake ever to hit Japan. It was a magnitude 9.0 quake. Within an hour, waves over 10 feet tall began to crash on the shores. For days, waves lashed against the coast. They destroyed buildings, bridges, and homes. The strongest waves were over 33 feet tall. Japan's tsunami warning system saved lives. Many people were able to escape to safety.

NUCLEAR FALLOUT

The Fukushima **nuclear** plant suffered a lot of damage because of the disasters. Harmful **radiation** leaked out into the air and water. People from the plant had to evacuate. They left their homes for safety reasons.

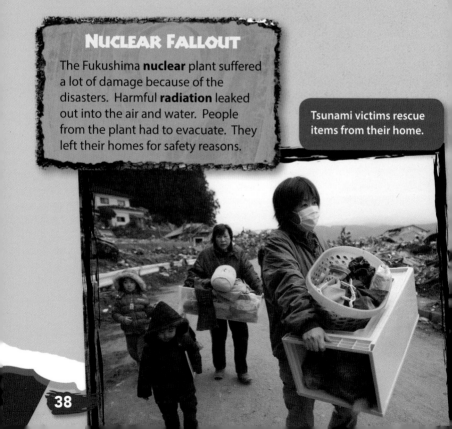

Tsunami victims rescue items from their home.

Tsunamis can carry large objects incredible distances.

LONG LASTING IMPACTS

In the days after the disaster, it was a challenge to get help to people. Many people in Japan had no way to communicate with their loved ones. They could not find their belongings, either. Water covered towns and coastal areas. Buildings were no longer standing. Many people were afraid to go back to their homes. They feared another earthquake.

THE RING OF FIRE

The Ring of Fire is a place on Earth's crust where many plates meet. Around 90 percent of all the earthquakes in the world happen there. It is home to 75 percent of the world's volcanoes. It is also where many of the most recent tsunamis have happened.

Indonesia
Indonesia has more active volcanoes than any other country in the world. This is because the island sits on top of four different plates. In 2004, it was struck by one of the worst tsunamis in history.

earthquakes

volcanoes

North America
The Juan de Fuca plate and the Pacific plate are crashing together. This motion built the Cascade mountains. And it's the reason Mount St. Helens erupted in 1980.

South America
The Nazca plate and the South American plate are colliding. This slow process made the Andes mountains. It also created the volcanoes Cotopaxi and Azul.

Famine and Drought

Terrible things can happen when there is too much water, but not having enough water can be just as deadly. Droughts are painfully dry periods that can scar the land and people for decades. When there isn't enough rain, soil becomes parched. Without water, the ground can't keep plants healthy and alive. The dry conditions can lead to **famine**. Droughts and famine often occur together, but they can also happen on their own. But famine is a disaster that can be prevented. And when we work together, no one needs to go without food.

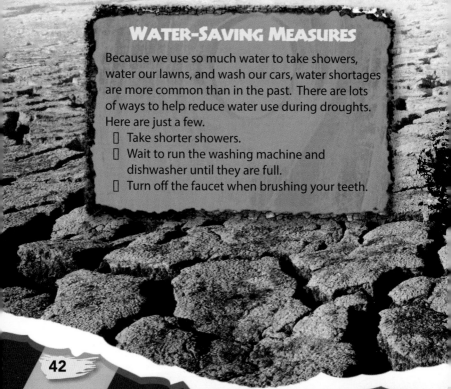

WATER-SAVING MEASURES

Because we use so much water to take showers, water our lawns, and wash our cars, water shortages are more common than in the past. There are lots of ways to help reduce water use during droughts. Here are just a few.

- Take shorter showers.
- Wait to run the washing machine and dishwasher until they are full.
- Turn off the faucet when brushing your teeth.

FAMINES

An earthquake or flood can happen in a flash. But a famine happens over time. Famine causes starvation. When crops don't grow and people don't get enough to eat, some time must pass before a person starves and dies. This also makes the consequences of famines preventable. Help can be sent before the situation gets too bad.

Simple grains such as rice may be used to feed those who are fighting for survival.

The Great Potato Famine

In the early 1800s, the people of Ireland fed their families with potatoes. Nearly half of the country lived on potatoes. But in the mid-1800s, disease struck the potato plants. The crops failed, and a great famine took hold. People had nothing to eat. Farmers had no way to make money. Over one million people died. Another million left Ireland to make their homes in places with more food. Many moved to the United States to make new lives for themselves.

A CHANGED IRELAND

Many things changed for Ireland as a result of The Great Potato Famine. People were angry that the government did not do more to help the people who were starving. They changed the laws to help the poor and hungry.

COMING TO AMERICA

The Great Potato Famine began a heavy wave of **immigration** to the United States. It started in the mid-1800s and lasted until the early 1900s. By 1921, Ireland had lost nearly half its population.

Heat Wave

Droughts can destroy the food supply system and make life a struggle, but heat waves can cause just as much damage. In 2003, a horrible heat wave hit Europe. The temperature was hotter than it had been in 500 years. Almost 30,000 people died. They didn't know how to deal with the heat. Because their bodies were weaker and more sensitive, the **elderly** were most affected. Cooling centers and local pools helped people survive.

DEHYDRATION

One major reason people die during heat waves is dehydration. Dehydration happens when the body does not get enough water. During a heat wave, the body sweats to cool off. But sweating causes the body to lose water. Drinking lots of water can prevent dehydration.

EUROPEAN SUMMER

The summers in most European countries are mild. Homes and buildings are often old and don't have great insulation. And since even hot summer months tend to have cool evenings, many homes and buildings don't have air conditioning. Without air conditioning, extreme heat can be hard to live through.

DISASTER FROM WITHIN

Sometimes, a disaster doesn't come from above us or below us. Sometimes, the disaster comes from inside us. Diseases can wipe out plants, animals, and people. Diseases spread in many ways. An **epidemic** occurs when a disease spreads throughout a wide area. But sometimes, diseases spread around the whole world. This is called a **pandemic**. In turn, scientists are discovering new ways to treat these threats. And people are finding new ways to thrive.

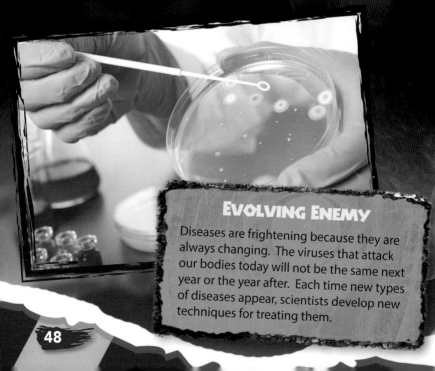

EVOLVING ENEMY

Diseases are frightening because they are always changing. The viruses that attack our bodies today will not be the same next year or the year after. Each time new types of diseases appear, scientists develop new techniques for treating them.

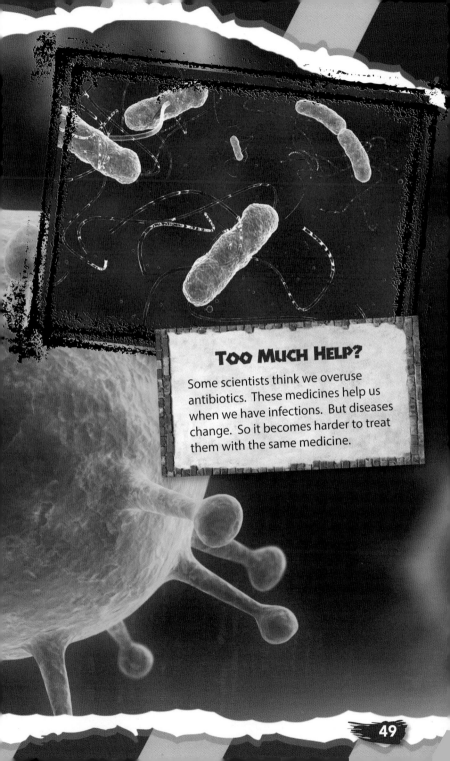

TOO MUCH HELP?

Some scientists think we overuse antibiotics. These medicines help us when we have infections. But diseases change. So it becomes harder to treat them with the same medicine.

The Black Death

Europe in the 1300s was haunted by an unforgettable disease. The Black Death spread through the land, causing terrible skin sores, cramps, fever, and weakness.

The disease began in rats and mice. These rodents carried fleas. With a bite, the fleas infected humans. Over 25 million people died. Mass graves were dug to bury hundreds, sometimes thousands of bodies.

RING AROUND THE ROSIE

Some people think the song *Ring Around the Rosie* comes from the time of the Black Death. During the plague, people placed roses and posies in their pockets and in the mouths of the dead to cover up the smell of the dead bodies.

PLAGUE PREVENTION

The Black Death is what people called the bubonic plague in the 1300s. Today, it is virtually nonexistent. If, by chance, someone gets it, doctors know how to treat it. They can even give people close to the infected person a **vaccine** to make sure it doesn't spread.

In the 1300s, doctors wore long robes and beaked masks as they visited patients infected with the plague.

A Frightening Flu

Pandemics are not a thing of the past. The 20th century hosted one of the worst pandemics in history. Between the years 1918 and 1920, over 500 million people across the world got the flu. The influenza pandemic began in the spring of 1918. Soldiers traveling between the United States and Europe during World War I spread the disease. The flu virus changed and hit in three waves. The second and third waves were deadlier than the first. By late 1919, the virus had killed between 20 and 40 million people around the world. Today, vaccines can prevent people from getting the flu. Today's flu vaccine and modern medicine are able to treat many illnesses quickly, easily, and safely.

AIRBORNE GERMS

Before air travel was common, most diseases were contained by oceans. Today, people can travel around the world in a single day. Planes can transport diseases quickly from one place to another. That makes it easier for a pandemic to break out.

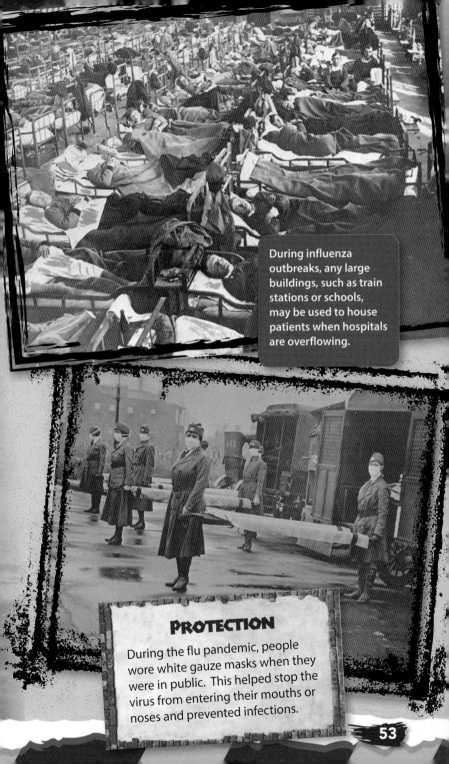

During influenza outbreaks, any large buildings, such as train stations or schools, may be used to house patients when hospitals are overflowing.

PROTECTION

During the flu pandemic, people wore white gauze masks when they were in public. This helped stop the virus from entering their mouths or noses and prevented infections.

PRESENT-DAY PANDEMICS

Officially known as *H1N1*, this virus is also called *swine flu* or *pig flu* because it appears to have spread from pigs to humans. This strain of influenza has many names, but they all describe a pandemic that hit the world in 2009. Within a single year, over 500,000 people died worldwide. Over 213 countries reported cases of swine flu. Doctors found ways to treat it by studying how it spread.

H1N1 2009 DEATHS

countries, territories, and areas with lab-confirmed cases and number of deaths as reported to World Health Organization

Reported Cases

•	1–10
•	11–50
●	51–500
⬤	501 and more
▢	Country/territory/area with confirmed cases

bird flu

human flu

Pigs can have more than one virus that mix to form a new virus.

Humans can catch swine flu by breathing in the virus.

swine flu

Humans can spread the virus to one another.

LEARNING FROM DISASTER

Nature can be as deadly as it is beautiful. Earthquakes, tsunamis, and fires are only some of the natural forces that have claimed lives. These disasters haunt us, but it's in the face of a disaster that we learn how strong we really are. Experts around the world are studying how to predict disasters and find new ways to rescue those who are in trouble. Because whatever the disaster, we will weather the storm together.

Scientists may learn more about how to predict the next disaster.

New medicines may be developed.

Bridges can be built stronger.

GLOSSARY

absorb—to soak up, to drink in

debris—the leftover pieces of something that has been destroyed

elderly—older people past middle age

engineers—people who use math and science to build things

epicenter—the place where an earthquake is the strongest

epidemic—the spread of a disease throughout a wide area

eruptions—violent sudden outbursts

evacuate—to remove from a place of danger

excess—related to too much of

famine—a lack of food that leads to starvation

geographical—to have to do with the natural characteristics of the world

immigration—coming to a country of which one is not a native

imminent—likely to occur at any moment

magma—the burning liquid inside a volcano before it erupts

magnitude—the measurement of an earthquake's strength

massive—huge in size, power, or strength

meteorologists—people who study the weather

meteors—objects moving through space at great speeds

nuclear—relating to energy created when atoms are split

pandemic—the spread of a disease throughout the world

plates—the huge movable segments into which the Earth's crust is divided

radiation—the process in which waves or pieces of energy are put out

storm surges—rises in water levels caused by a storm

thawed—melted

tidal waves—powerful and destructive waves that are much larger than normal

tsunami—a huge wave of water created by an earthquake

vaccine—substances given to people or animals to protect against particular diseases

INDEX

BIBLIOGRAPHY

Cunningham, Kevin. *Pandemics (True Books).*
Children's Press, 2011.
   Read terribly true stories of sickness and disaster and how
   people recovered from these unforgettable pandemics.

Grace, Catherine O'Neill. *Forces of Nature:*
The Awesome Power of Volcanoes, Earthquakes, and
Tornadoes. **National Geographic Children's Books,**
2004.
   Learn how powerful Mother Nature really is. You will get
   up close and personal with these natural disasters through
   spectacular images, detailed diagrams, and pages packed
   with facts.

Tarshis, Lauren. *I Survived Hurricane Katrina, 2005.*
Scholastic Paperbacks, 2011.
   This story about a boy, his dog, and a terrible storm brings
   Hurricane Katrina to life. Find out how Barry will survive after
   he is swept away from his family by the floodwaters. At the end
   of this book, there is a question-and-answer section about this
   horrific storm.

Watts, Claire. *Natural Disasters (Eyewitness Books).*
DK Children, 2006.
   From tsunamis to avalanches, a wide range of natural disasters
   are covered in this book. You'll even find a discussion on
   disasters that may happen in the future. This book perfectly
   combines the fascinating and frightening aspects of natural
   disasters.

MORE TO EXPLORE

Volcano Hazards Program
http://volcanoes.usgs.gov

This site is erupting with volcanic information! There is a map of the major United States volcanoes, a photo glossary, webcams, pictures, and movies of volcanoes, all from the United States Geological Survey.

Weather Wiz Kids
http://www.weatherwizkids.com

Visit this site to learn facts about weather and natural disasters, what causes them, and how to stay safe during and after these amazing events.

The Great Plague
http://history.parkfieldict.co.uk/stuarts/the-great-plague

The plague killed nearly one-third of Europeans during the Middle Ages. Find out just how awful this disease was and the crazy ways people tried to cure themselves.

Be Prepared in Every Situation
http://www.ready.gov/kids

Be ready for just about any disaster with the information on this site. You'll find facts about disasters, how to make a plan, what you need for a readiness kit, and games and activities.

ABOUT THE AUTHOR

Tamara Leigh Hollingsworth was born and raised in Cupertino, California. She attended Hollins University, an all women's college, in Roanoke, Virginia, where she earned a degree in English. While in college, she spent time traveling through Europe where she visited a memorial to the great potato famine. For the majority of her life since then, she has been a high school English teacher. She currently lives in Atlanta, Georgia. When she's not working with her beloved students, Tamara loves to spend time with her husband, her daughter, her books, and her iPod.